Mrugtrishna ~ मृगतृष्णा

The never ending thirst of life's quest!

Shruti Sharma

BookLeaf Publishing
India | USA | UK

Made with ❤ on the BookLeaf Publishing Platform
www.bookleafpub.in
www.bookleafpub.com

Dedication

I dedicate this book to my inner child. I am taking all the measures to satisfy your curious heart little Shruti!!
We are sharing our thoughts with the world now!! I dedicate this book to my mom too for sharing this form of art with me and making it more special for us.

Preface

Let me introduce myself a bit before you go through the pages of my first poetry book!!

Namaste! My name is Shruti, I belong to Lucknow, Uttar Pradesh. I am a graduate in Bachelor of Arts, and I hold a Post Grad. Diploma in Creative Writing as well & my favorite subject has always been literature, that's why I think I felt the urge of choosing 'A book' as the medium to convey my thoughts and feelings.

All these poems are a part of my heart, my feelings and my experiences through this journey of my life.

These poems are written through years, since my teenage till now. So, with this book I am sharing a piece of myself with you all!! I am still a beginner so kindly ignore the mistakes and catch the emotion.

I will be more than happier if anyone found it relatable and interesting!!

Like I mentioned earlier I enjoy literature, so this book is a collection of my poems in both, English and Hindi.

I hope all my readers enjoy this book more than me!! ;)

Acknowledgements

I am grateful for this life and every single person who has been a part of my life in different phases and in different roles.
I learnt a lot from everyone and in some way, you have all helped me in becoming the person, that I am today!!
So, Thank you for all the lessons and encouragement and all the love!!

1. The Last flower.

Old faces came knocking at my door,
Searching for the girl who lived here before?
I said, she's been gone for a while,
I think, she was sent into exile!
for what? they asked?
Her crime was being a giver!!
hence, she bled until she was empty,
While loving people who wished her misery.
What a fool to think, it was love? hah!
Don't bother to wait for her return.
She is no more your concern.
the little girl is happy in her exile,
at peace, content with no more trial.
I banged the door & threw the key,
As my inner child is now safe with me!

2. हिस्सा

एक हिस्सा कहीं खो गया है दिल का
जो ढूंढे मिलता नहीं,
हर अक्स में तलाशा उसको पर
रंग, रूप मिलता नहीं,

पतझड़ सी उम्मीद मेरी बटोर,
हिम्मत जुटाती हूँ,
कहीं ये तो नहीं?
फिर सोचके, कदम बढ़ाती हूँ....

अब तो शब्द भी सूख गए इस इन्तज़ार में,
इश्क की सियाही जो खत्म हो गयी इस बाज़ार में!
न इसका, न उसका जाने किसका है ?
जो खो दिया मैंने, मेरे दिल का हिस्सा है।

3. Hidden World

A world, hidden, once we held dear to our heart,
Created and concealed, when we were six or four,
Love laid its foundation, warmth builds the wall,
innocence carved the windows, probity painted the door,
Our magical world, we shared with the first friend,
when our heart skipped the beat on the knock of our
first love!
Life was full of colors & happiness has no end.
until betrayal cracked the window & we were forced to
unlove!
the first kick of maturity, taught us pain & insecurity,
we locked our magic in a box and the world got razed.
deep in the sea of fear, we lost the golden key,
Do you miss it too, our lost world that's now full of
haze?
The magical world, hidden deep in the ocean of senility.

4. Desired Love?

What do you desire?
Love or pleasure.
A temporary moment of lust or
a reciprocation of forever?
An ordinary attraction or
a cosmic treasure?
Karmic connections or
a red thread binding us together?
The betrayal of selfishness or
a selfless bond to share?
Supreme power of alignment or
a war of what's fair?
A diligent walk to the healthy future or
a race to lonely stairs?
A home filled with love or
a market full of spares.
You think you play well but our,
Universe is 'The Ultimate Player'.
Sit, pick one, what your heart's real Desire!

5. Human or a Program?

I'm alive! My heart's beating.
What I feel?
Not peace but like a new software is downloading,
Programing my mind & feelings,
to face the world and the situations uncanny.
It does feels like a battle!
A war with my real self & the broken rattle.
The society's right ways of reacting,
Like I said Yes, my heart's racing.
A functional course of learning,
what should a woman need, desire or be creating.
I own the power of my fertility, but who's regulating?
Do I want a new life? But others are debating!
Should I fight back or stay mum like a manikin?
Yes, yes, I'm alive! My heart's beating.

6. What if ?

What if I stopped waiting?
Will you find your way through the long closed doors?
What if I'm tired & not strong enough to hold it anymore?
Will you run for me to embrace my soul?
What if my belief is fainting away like my breath every day?
Will you caress my hair and gently reap my heart's hole?
What if I need you to hold me & never let me go?
Will you dare to cross the borders just to see me for night?
What if I lost my hope?
Will you bring in a new ray of light?
What if I say, the patience of wait is killing me inside,
Will you die in me, to keep me alive?

7. Hopeless romantic

Hopeless romance is my core.
Isn't it romantic when the night awaits the moon?
Trees singing with the wind,
spotting sunset by the dune!
A glowing pair of swans dancing in the lake?
Eager spring waiting for the first bloom.
Flower petals falling from the trees,
painting world like a rainbow, as far as you tune.
Empty roads shining with Komorebi,
Sunrise from the hill, adieu by the noon,
Is it too much to adore?
or Do I sound like a fool?
Sorry can't deny anymore,
No doubt I am a hopeless romantic for sure!!

8. A dream came true!

Dreamt of my encounter on an island with a king.
It was smooth as The Universe pulled its strings.
He felt like a gentle breeze,
A warm home with candles lit,
Carrying a crescent moon in his palms,
Ohh...his scent makes me calm!
Jasmine never tasted this sweet before,
his warm hug, made me crave a little more?
When he pulled me close under the starry night,
So, can we kiss on a tunnel ride?
Doe eyes sparkling with the look of love,
fluttering hearts, can't get enough!
A funny bone with a runny nose,
How I wish this dream to come true!!

9. सार

जितना चाहो छूटेगा ही,
ये जीवन है, तो रूठेगा ही।

बस एक हठ यही था मेरा,
प्रीतम हर संग, रास न रचाए!!
पर प्रेम को किसने बाँधा है?
मन को ये कैसे समझायें?
मुरली भी सौतन लागे जिसको,
उसे सांझा करना कैसे भाए?
भोली थी, अभिमानी थी पर,
प्रीतम की दीवानी थी,
तो, प्रेम ही खोया, प्रेम ही पाया,
टूटकर भी एक नया रूप अपनाया,
ये सार समझ तब आया,
जीवन पलछिन सांझ सवेरा,
ना कुछ तेरा, ना कुछ मेरा।।

10. विरक्तिमय

धरती ही जब है काँप उठी,
तो सृष्टी कहाँ रचाओगे?
हे त्रिगुण शक्ति, स्वामी दाता,
शक्ति किस जगह चलाओगे?
जन जन ही हुआ विरक्तिमय,
भक्तिमय किसे बनाओगे?
निष्ठा दर दर मारी फिरती,
किसे सत्य का राग सुनाओगे?

कर्तव्यों का कोई मोल नहीं,
अधिकार का उठता ऊँचा स्वर!!
बेइमान का कॉलर ऊँचा है,
ईमान झुकाए फिरता सिर!
आत्मा विहीन दानव ढूँढें;
किस देह में बाकी रक्त बूंद।।

11. बिखरे स्वप्न

दम तोड़ते चेहरे पर,
दम तोड़ती मुसकान,
दम तोड़ती जागृति,
दम तोड़ती पेहचान,
दम तोड़ती अभिव्यक्ति,
दम तोड़ता इंसान,
हर भाव जिसमें अपना खम छोड़ रहा है,
वो शख्स धीरे धीरे दम तोड़ रहा है!
क्या हमारी कलपनाओं की ताबीर यही थी?
क्या आजके इंसान की तस्वीर यही थी??

12. Partner in Crime

Ma once said~
Your souls are intertwined,
No matter where you go, he will run behind,
As your souls are determined!!

No doubt why, you saved me so many times!!
slowly-slowly, sneaking out of the line...
you taught me how to break the rules,
rebel ~ before I lose my mind!

I could chase my dreams as I knew,
You will catch me, whenever I fly...
You came as my brother, but you are my child.
The one who I love the most,
apple of my eye.....
protecting me from afar or by my side,
The guy who never gave up on me ~ Mera Bhai!

13. Two sides of a Coin

Brave for you, maybe 'coward' for others?
strong for you yet 'fragile' for others?
Good for you but 'terrible' to others?
Comforting for you but 'annoying' for others?
Peace for you but 'chaos' for others?
Gift for you but 'too much' for others?
Giver for you but 'selfish' for others?
no matter what you do,
nothing matters!
it's a coin with two sides,
One is worst and one is better!
Life is just perspective.
once sweet, once bitter!!

14. Sister, My soulmate!

Among murmuring of hundreds,
a silent heart sits still.
fingers fidgeting through papers,
eyes drifting through people,
a calm voice broke the shield,
she walked with me through storms,
shared my sorrow, held me close in her arms,
she felt my heart like I felt her pain,
promised to walk together even in rain,
we don't share blood but intuition,
we share love and reciprocation!
My silent heart found a mate,
I found my sister, my soulmate.

15. Fine!

The world seems 'Fine'!
People seem sweet and shine,
Pictures are perfect and lit,
Until you talk and sit,
everyone who was fine, is sick!
Sick of life and struggles,
Sick of heartbreak and juggle,
Sick of the chase for money,
tired of being 'a honey',
generational trauma and fear of love,
incompetency, feeling like a used glove,
but when you ask? It's 'Fine!'
the world, seemed happier is dying!!

16. Femi~masculine.

They want her feminine,
but expect her to lift everything on her shoulders,
They like her dependent,
but want her to handle the world boulder,
They respect her when covered,
but enjoy her secretly as a slaveholder,
They make her weak,
but want her to work as a stakeholder,
They took away her powers,
but want her to serve them like a clot molder,
They push her to edges,
yet make her masculine like a petty smolder!!

17. Over sensitive?

He said you feel too much!!
'Don't act like a child!'

Her world fell on her feet,
a shadow crawled back on her mind.
She trusted him with her life,
she told him all her secrets and acted like his wife,
She felt safe, loved and important,
hence got scared when he felt distant!
She painted her world around him,
He is the sun, the moon and her prince charming!
She was sure of his potential of handling her at her worst,
hence, she loved him with her best, for her it was a must!
She forgot who she was, her worth, her stature,
He shoved the mirror on her face, compared her with a hooker.
She asked for love and time, he felt annoyed,
Scolded her; 'Don't act like a child!'
He pushed her back in her past,
where monsters of trauma haunted her heart!
Yes! she felt too much, cause she held too much,
She walked past you and hell yeah, earned too much!
You still live the same, she is shining like a flame.

Powerful and wiser, embraced her inner child & made a name!

18. Love of Silence

Can you hear my silence?
and read my eyes?
observe my gestures?
I met a lot of you and the ones who pester!

Just sit with me and feel the breeze,
say nothing, stare the trees,
birds singing by the lake,
Can you love without any give & take?

will you learn to love with no physicality?
being together far away from reality,
will you feel what I feel?
look at me with love and zeal!

Will you not change with time?
but grow with me?
Will you still listen to my silence,
when you get to have all of me?

19. माँ

मेरा प्रथम भी वो, मेरा अंत भी वो
कि हर आहट पर जो दौड़े,
मेरा सर्वस्व भी वो,
पहली धड़कन से आख़िरी तक,
मेरा प्रारब्ध है वो,
मेरे एक अश्रु पे जो विध्वंसक करें विश्व का,
मेरा आदि भी वो, अनंत भी वो,
मेरी जननी भी वो, मेरी करनी भी वो
मेरा मान भी वो, सम्मान भी वो
है कहने को तो माँ पर मेरा अस्तित्व है वो॥

20. मृगतृष्णा

मन प्राण दुखित, सर्वांग तृषित
जीवन कैसा दुर्भेद लक्ष्य?
जिस पर मन प्राण समर्पित थे,
कब जाना था वह “यक्ष प्रश्न”?
जीवन वीणा को खनकाती,
वो साँस भी है अब श्राप ग्रसित!
जिसको मैंने जाना समझा,
वह जीवन था आल्हाद रहित,
मन गर्वित था जिस शक्ति पर,
वह हुई है अब आधार रहित।
सब भ्रमित, तृषित, सब थकित चकित,
फिर किस पर मन गर्वीला है ?
जिस पर मन- प्राण प्रफुल्लित थे,
मृगतृष्णा का उड़ान खटोला है॥

21. धवल चंद्रिका

यूँ धवल चंद्रिका मुस्काती,
निशि आंगन में खिलती जाती,
मन विरहन को शीतल करती,
जब पुष्प चंदनिया बरसाती,
महका सा धरती का आँचल,
महका-महका सा गगन बाग,
महकी सी चहुँ दिशाएँ हैं ।
महकी प्रिय की वह मधुर याद।
जब रात ये महकी-महकी है,
तो सुबह भी महकेगी खिलकर,
जब विरह का मौसम पावन है,
प्रिय मिलन बहुत होगा सुखकर॥